Blockchain

The Industry Leader's Guide to Blockchain, Understanding Bitcoin and Entering the Digital Economy

Inside Success Today

Table of Contents

Introduction

I want to thank you and congratulate you for downloading *Blockchain: The Industry Leader's Guide to Blockchain, Understanding Bitcoin and Entering the Digital Economy.*

Like many, as Bitcoin rose to prominence just a few short years ago, I was interested in the ideas communicated behind the first major cryptocurrency but decided to stay on the sidelines. Within a short time, this one cryptocurrency climbed in value to new highs each and every month. I would look at how much a single Bitcoin was trading for and think to myself: 'I wish I had invested earlier'. Two years ago, and after reading about the emergence of additional digital cryptocurrencies, I concluded that there is still money to be made. Today, in the year 2017, I'm proud to say that there are still lots of profit left on the table for those that wish to enter the economy of digital currencies. In the grand scheme of things, we are still in the very early stages of cryptocurrencies, and now is a very good time to enter if your interest is to turn digital currencies into profit for you and your family.

The intention of this book is to give you a summary on the world of cryptocurrencies, and to provide you with all of the basic information that you need to get invested and start realizing profit as soon as possible. The cost of investment is entirely up to you, with starting investments as low as just a few hundred dollars. Even this might seem like a hefty investment, but in just a few short months you will see that a minimal investment can create a large amount of wealth.

Nothing is easy, and nothing is free – you know this as well as I do, and it was the reason why I was so skeptical about entering this market. The truth is that the reason more people have not adopted digital currencies is because the barrier to entry is one based on knowledge. Like with computer programming, there is a basic set of knowledge that you must first obtain to be able to compete with other traders and make money through creating/buying and selling digital currencies. I aim to explain everything you need to know in simple and clear terms, and by the end of this book you will have a clear game plan for how to enter the market and start making money as soon as possible.

We are the precipice of a revolution in the way the world treats monetary policy as a whole. There will be rapid changes in the coming years, and you will want to be an early adopter of what is sure to be a great source of income for the few that decided to learn about the digital economy and get a head start. There are other resources available to you, but many of these sources are convoluted and focus on the wrong aspects of digital currencies. My goal is to teach you the premise and for you to understand the mechanics in a way that leads to profit.

Continue reading and you will discover the secret underground economy arising in the form of cryptocurrencies. The technology might seem complicated; it might appear out of your area of expertise, but the truth is that this niche market is not that difficult to understand, and with my explanations you will have a clear picture of how the digital economy works today, how to profit from it, and where it is going in the future.

Inside Success Today

Chapter 1: The Fundamentals of Blockchain

Blockchain as an Argument for the Gold Standard

The basic premise for why blockchain was created lies in an argument that has been going back and forth since the Untied States changed a fundamental aspect of their monetary policy; the switch from the gold standard to a faith based economy. In the early 20th century, the United States relied on a gold backed economy. It is the type of economy that nation states have relied on for millennia. It is the simplest form to back currencies, and can be quite easily understood. The basic premise is that each dollar you have in your pocket represents some portion of gold kept by the United States. In fact, up until a little over one hundred years ago, you could exchange your U.S. currency for the equivalent in gold. Conversely you could trade gold in for currency, in addition to the option of selling the gold. It is a simplistic view on how currencies work, and nations could grow more economically viable by gaining possession of a larger sum of gold. This premise was a major motivator for nations to expand their wealth and even promoted the discovery of the Americas.

The 20th century, with its advancing economy with many distinct layers of investment and financial markets, proved to be too much for the gold standard to bear. The Great Depression of the 1930s showed the world that a gold backed economy is simplistic, but leaves lots of discretion on inflation out of the hands of the government. This one event was the catalyst for the forty-year move to abandon the gold standard. Today, the dollar in your pocket is worth a dollar because you believe it is worth one dollar. There is no gold stored anywhere to back the value of the dollar, and it is in fact the intermingling of economies that give strength to the currency that we hold. This allows for government intervention in case of financial crises, but also gives the power of inflation and other monetary decisions to the government. There are a few who see this as a form of corruption, or at least opening the doorway to possible corruption in the future.

I wanted to start with the gold standard, because at its core, that is what cryptocurrencies like Bitcoin represent; they are the digital incarnation of the gold standard. The promise of the gold standard is to leave inflation out of the hands of human intervention. The Great Depression proved this to be disaster for millions of Americans, yet the basic premise for how inflation would be handled is quite sound. Gold is finite, and yet new gold deposits are found year over year. The amount of gold that enters the economy starts at a large rate as there are many deposits to be found, and gradually slows over time. This is the exact model that digital currencies follow for how they enter the market. The start of Bitcoin opened the floodgates of the digital currency, with new Bitcoins being created at the fastest rate in its history. These coins have grown to become worth more and more as it has become more difficult to 'mine' new coins. This explains both the natural deflation of gold, and also why Bitcoin has grown in value. As new coins enter the market at slower rates over time, the value of all existing coins gain in value.

Blockchain currencies have evolved and are handled slightly differently than being modeled directly after gold, but at their core this is the system that they are trying to represent. By creating a digital version of a finite resource, a currency is created that cannot be tainted by human intervention. It is a libertarian's dream in how human actors cannot change the underlying value of a currency. It cannot be created at will to stem inflation, and the currency cannot suddenly be changed to restrict older coins. It is a currency that is at the mercy of the algorithm that created it, and the mining of gold is the model that it follows.

Blockchain then is the underlying technology that allows for this system to exist. If the hope and ideals of the creator and contributors of blockchain technology is to create economies with little human intervention, then they have done an admirable job of making it so that it in all aspects it follows this model. As you continue reading, keep in mind the ideals and goals of what the creators of blockchain wanted to accomplish. It was an open source project to take power away from government backed currencies, and to restore that power to the natural economy of supply and demanded. Modeled after gold and based on the ideals of traditional currency backing, blockchain used incredibly advanced mechanics to facilitate a model of this natural process.

Modeling the Mechanics of Blockchain

Knowing that blockchain is modeled after a gold backed economy illustrates the premise for how inflation is set to work over the coming decades and it demonstrates what the creators of blockchain wanted to accomplish, but it does little to explain the actual mechanics of blockchain. To understand the underpinning technology of blockchain, let me walk you through a simple example. Blockchain, at its core, is technology that allows for the asynchronous transmission of data, and does not allow any individual human actors to tamper with the creation or deletion of data. This may sound like a complicated explanation, but if you think about blockchain as a special piece of paper, it actually becomes quite simple.

Imagine that you and two friends have three sheets of magic paper. You have one, as well as each of your friends. What makes this piece of paper so incredible is that when information is written one sheet of paper, it magically gets transmitted to *all* the sheets of paper. In addition, it is impossible to erase or cross out anything that is written on these sheets of paper; information is permanent and cannot be destroyed. You and your friends use these magical sheets of paper to keep track of how much money is owed between the three of you. For example, if you owe your first friend $30, you would write this debt on the sheet of paper. The knowledge of this debt is therefore shared between all three members. When you pay off the debt, you write down that the debt has been paid. The genius of this is that since all party members know the information that is being recorded, it is impossible to manipulate any one sheet of paper. You cannot cross out the debt to a friend because your friend would be made aware, but in addition the second friend would also be made aware. There is no transaction or storage of data that does not become clear to all members of the group.

In this scenario, no one member has enough clout to manipulate the information stored on the sheets of paper. For information to be recorded and accepted as 'true', two of the three members would have to agree. In our example, the debt from you to the first friend can only be wiped away if the first and second friends agree that the debt has been paid. Imagine the incentive structure here if all members of this group were only looking out for the best possible outcome for themselves. You would like to wipe away the debt on your sheet so that you do not have to pay your friend; this might be a rotten move but it is the best financial outcome. The first friend would like to keep the debt so that he or she can ask for a second payment of $30. For the third friend though, they are a neutral party. Their interest lies in themselves, who has no part in this transaction. Their driving interest would be to ensure that the magic sheets of paper are accurate, so that they can use this same resource in the future. Therefore, the only way that the debt could actually be wiped away is if the second friend witnesses you giving the first friend the $30 that is owed. After this transaction has taken place and the second friend witnesses the transaction, the debt can be wiped away. It is still in the interest of the first friend to keep the debt, however he would be outvoted in terms of changing the document, with two out of three party members agreeing that the debt has been paid.

This is the heart of blockchain, to have an open and clear transmission of data that does not give any single party information that all other parties do not also have. If you think about the three magic sheets of paper and extrapolate that to thousands of sheets of paper, you can start to see the beauty of what blockchain technology offers. Hundreds of people that have no relation to each other, and no inherent trust in each other, can suddenly communicate and clear transactions without worrying about one member cheating any other member. The cheating is impossible because every other member knows each and every action of all other members.

How Blockchain Technology *Actually* Works

The magic sheets of paper example will only take us so far in explaining the technology that powers cryptocurrencies. To truly understand how cryptocurrencies work, we need to get a bit more technical. This is arguably the hardest part of this book to understand, but it is worth internalizing the fundaments of the blockchain system. To start, we need to imagine our magic sheet of paper as a large public ledger. That is, it is a large accounting book that everyone has access to. Anyone can change what is written in the ledger, but all readers of the ledger would have access to this change. The beauty of this ledger is that a majority of readers of the ledger would have to agree to any and all changes.

The ledger is essentially a very long list of all transactions that have taken place between all members that have access to the ledger. This forms part of the 'chain' in blockchain. The chain is a list of every single transaction that has taken place over time. In the example with the magic paper, we saw that the debt from you to one of your friends could not be wiped away unless a majority of the holders of the paper agreed that the debt had been paid. In essence, that is what this blockchain ensures. It is a recording of every single transaction ever made, but transactions are only recorded if a majority of members agree that the transaction took place. In this way, no single member can manipulate the book to game the system. Other members would disagree with the changes to the ledger, and the changes would not get recorded.

This is the theory of blockchain, but in practice the functionality is slightly different. Working with the most established currency, Bitcoin, let's review how a simple purchase is made. Suppose that you have one Bitcoin, and you want to make a purchase from an online retailer that costs half of that Bitcoin. You have two forms of identification on this system, a 'public' and 'private' key. You would tell the retailer your public key, and verify with the system that you indeed own that Bitcoin by providing your private key. The retailer would look at this public key and see it as if you were opening your wallet and showing that you have the cash on hand to make the purchase. Anyone that has both the public and private key can make a transaction, so think about ownership of both of these keys as essentially having full access to your wallet – a public key lets you see the contents of the wallet, a private key lets you move the contents of the wallet. The transaction between you and the retailer is then stored as a single block of data. All members of the Bitcoin system would have to confirm that the money has been moved from your wallet to the wallet of the retailer. You were able to move this half a Bitcoin because you had access to your private and public key, and also the public key of the retailer.

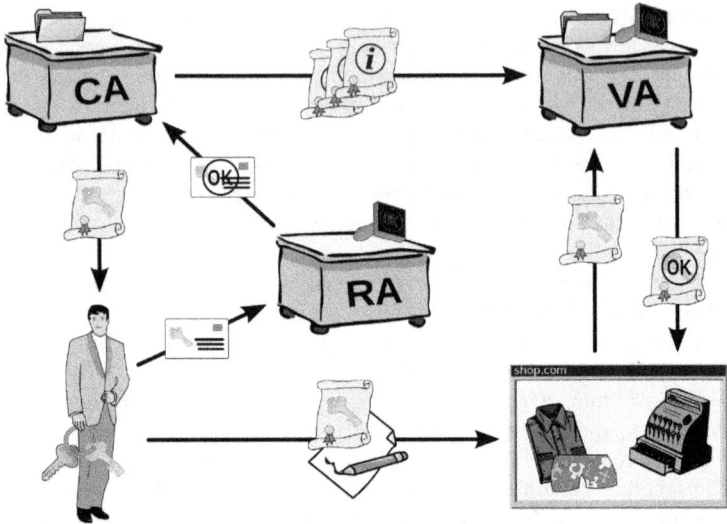

Photo Courtesy of Wikimedia

The diagram above demonstrates this principle of how blockchain works. While there are minor differences in terms of programming or exactly how new coins are created, this idea of a public and private key for your wallet, as well as a confirmation from all members that trade coins, is a basic premise of blockchain technology as a whole.

To understand the larger picture, simply know the goal of blockchain – to decentralize the transmission of currency but to have even greater security with each transaction. There was no bank in this transaction; there was no payment processor. This was a transaction between two parties, yourself and the retailer, and yet you had the assurance of thousands of Bitcoin users that the transaction took place. As time has passed since I entered into cryptocurrencies, I have developed a newfound appreciation for how this technology works. You have to keep in mind that not only did every single person view this transaction, but that this transaction was still entirely private. Even though the transaction was recorded and confirmed by all members in the network, no one knows who actually went through with the transaction. They are unaware of both the receiver and transmitter of the Bitcoin. You must also understand what looking at the whole blockchain can show. Many transactions from now, you can look at the blockchain and see this transaction that has taken place. In fact you can trace the very creation of the Bitcoin that you traded, and look at every single transaction that took place before it arrived in your wallet. There can be no disagreement about debts; money cannot be lost; it is perfect accountability that is also anonymous – it is in these ideas that make blockchain such an incredible technological force.

Chapter 2: Understanding The Appeal Of Cryptocurrencies

There are many reasons why cryptocurrencies have gained such widespread appeal in recent years. These advantages are both ideological and practical, and depending on your viewpoint of economies and the role of the government and anonymity, cryptocurrencies might align quite exactly with your ideal goals for any currency. There are many advantages that cryptocurrencies have over traditional government backed currencies, but before diving into that, I wanted to get one point out of the way; the main issue with digital currencies today is the extreme fluctuation in price and the number of places where digital currencies can be used. It is true that Bitcoin cannot be used to buy groceries, and it cannot be used to write a check or pay taxes. These are limitations due to how new these currencies are. What this chapter discusses is the *inherent* advantages that blockchain technology provides to digital currencies, and how the mechanics of blockchain offer a greater level of security than traditional forms of currency.

A Currency Controlled by the People

I decided to open this book with a short history of U.S. monetary policy as it relates to the gold standard. Many of the first adopters of cryptocurrencies are at the intersection of technology and libertarian ideals. This is the first reason that drew many to become interested in cryptocurrencies. They saw a currency free from government regulation; an anonymous currency that put the power of money back in the hands of those that owned it, and away from those that issued it. Aside from being modeled on a system that some people prefer, there are real inherent advantages to blockchain currencies; advantages that anyone from anywhere on the ideological spectrum can take advantage of.

The lack of government intervention in a currency is a major reason why people came to believe in cryptocurrencies as an idea. I definitely do not share some of the sentiments of many of the die-hard advocates of blockchain currencies, but it is hard to argue with some of the key points. Government intervention in currencies is very much a real concern. Three distinct examples come to mind; the 2008 financial crisis and the quantitative easing that took place afterwards, the recent change in banning several notes of currency in India and the rise of inflation in several poorer countries, namely Venezuela and Zimbabwe.

The 2008 financial crisis saw the United States Federal Reserve take some of the most drastic actions in its history. Aside from lowering interest rates to zero and providing the outlined structure for why a bailout is necessary to the largest banks that helped create the crisis, they also took part in quantitative easing for a number of years after the crisis. Quantitative easing is a fancy term for pumping cash into the economy. I separate this from inflation because the way in which the Fed handled this was actually quite clever, but still devious. They provided cash on hand to large banks to put on their ledgers. This ensured that day to day operations could be run, money could be lent and the economy would continue to function. In essence, the Fed was propping up banks that would have fallen to the wayside under different conditions. It is the opinion of many that the banks should not have been given this type of help. It was essentially government increasing the rate of inflation and hiding the effects by hiding the money within the major banks. Cryptocurrencies would allow for this, because their form of currency cannot be created at will. Also, transactions of this size, even if the government had the money on hand, could not be made without the entire public being made aware. Part of the issue with quantitative easing was just how secret it was at the time. Cryptocurrencies open up a level of transparency that is just not currently had with any government backed currency.

Second on the list of government intervention being a cause to rally behind cryptocurrencies is that certain notes can be made non-legal tender over night. In 2016, the Indian government decided that to combat counterfeit banks notes they would make certain commonly counterfeited notes non-legal tender. For many, this proved to be a real shock and destroyed the savings for many Indian families. If you had a large number of notes that were made non -legal tender, the money that you had on hand would have essentially vanished. This is an extreme case in modern times, but as you can imagine, the value of these notes plummeted right away. It became clear the government could not substitute an adequate number of bills, and overnight there was a run on many shops. Consumers were racing to spend the notes before they would be rendered useless.

Lastly, and a major factor for the creation of cryptocurrencies to begin with, comes the issue of government sponsored inflation. This is a real driving point for many early adopters of blockchain currencies. Since cryptocurrencies are based off of the model of gold, the government cannot inject lots of money into the economy and promote inflation. There are times when this is advantageous to be sure, but taking the power of printing money away from the government has its benefits. Humans are fallible, and therefore the government is fallible, and they can make mistakes in regards to how much they try and inflate the value of their backed currency. Look to Zimbabwe or Venezuela and you can see exactly this problem. The government of each country has produced too many bank notes, albeit with the honest intention of trying to steer the economy in the right direction. What they have ended up doing is taking the economy and ruining it. Cryptocurrencies would not suffer from this problem because there would be no opportunity for a government to have this power of manipulation to begin with.

Digital Cash

The simplest argument in favor of cryptocurrencies is that they function as a form of digital cash. In chapter one, I illustrated how a purchase would take place between a retailer and private citizen using Bitcoin. This purchase is most analogous to walking into a store and paying cash. It is the reason that for illegal services, such as purchasing narcotics online, Bitcoin and other cryptocurrencies are the only type of payment accepted. It is the digital form of cash. It cannot be traced back to the provider of the money, and there are no notes or statements about what the payment was for. It is the closest that we have come to a form of digital currency that functions much the same way as paper. Consider this in comparison to the credit cards that you use today.

All credit card transactions must go through third party payment processors. They payment processors have become an integral third party in the transmission of funds between two parties. They witness the transaction, have the identity of who completed the transaction, and are the single determining factor of whether or not the transaction goes through. Visa, MasterCard and other payment processors also skim money from this transaction, as it there business model to receive a percentage of the total transaction. It is essentially how they are paid for the service of completing the payment. By having cryptocurrencies bypass this, it reduces the transaction cost by lowering the overhead of moving money from one party to another. It also goes to further the notion that cryptocurrencies are anonymous, and yet totally visible to all. Everyone knows the transaction has taken place and it allows for the verification that the money has been moved. They function just like a payment processor, and yet the identity of the two parties that sent the payments is only known to the two themselves.

Security

In the early 1990s, it was predicted that the internet could never become a place to buy merchandise and services because there was no safe way to pay for goods. While we have come a long way since then, and are able to make relatively secure payments, however nothing is as safe as what cryptocurrencies offer. Think about the fact that all retailers that you have shopped online at have a stored record of that purchase. With that record is your name, what you purchased and your payment details, such as your credit card number. With Bitcoin and other cryptocurrencies, these transactions are ethereal. They happen at the moment that they take place and can never be revisited to verify specific details. Your identity is not stored and neither are your payment details. The only way that someone can commit fraud with a cryptocurrency is if they had access to both your private key and public key. This is the equivalent of someone snatching your wallet. Therefore, cryptocurrencies are the safest form of digital transmission of money, and are at least as secure as a physical item that you store on your person. This is a driving factor in the appeal of cryptocurrencies, and is why so many people have flocked to them. They offer a level of security completing unrivaled by credit cards and other forms of payment over the internet. In many ways, since there is added assurance that the funds have been transmitted, it might prove to be a better form of payment than cash itself.

Speculation

The value of the U.S. dollar is relative. It is relative to all of the other currencies in the world, and the power of the dollar cannot be taken on its own terms. It must always be measured in comparison to another world currency. Perhaps you are familiar with FOREX markets, or the foreign exchange markets for currencies. This is where traders buy and sell currencies to manipulate their values. This form of speculation serves the purpose of creating profit for traders of currencies, but for also correcting the value of the currency of one nation to the currency of another. The problem is that the value of your dollar is at the hands of traders that only care to make a profit for themselves based on the constant shifting value of the world's currencies. This is a scary idea, and cryptocurrencies can't be manipulated in the same way.

An argument for cryptocurrencies bypassing currency speculation is an odd one to make in 2017. After all, the main cause of concern for many analysts is that cryptocurrencies are highly speculative. This is because most blockchain based currencies can't be used for goods and services. Right now, the value of cryptocurrencies lies in the fact that they appreciate so quickly. This speculation is due to the fact that the best use of any cryptocurrencies today is to simply hold on to them. As their value as actual forms of making purchases increases, meaning more established accept payment by way of cryptocurrencies, this rampant speculation should cease. While cryptocurrencies may escape this speculation, traditional currencies will forever be intertwined with speculation from investors; FOREX trading will persist as long as there are multiple currencies backed by different governments. Cryptocurrencies have this advantage, if only in theory, in that the value of the currency is determined by the natural flow of that currency from mining, and not from other factors like private speculators.

Chapter 3: Planning Your Entry into Blockchain Currencies

You have a good understanding of the basics of how cryptocurrencies work and the appeal of these currencies. Now it's time to approach how you can make real money through cryptocurrencies. To start, I need to be frank about the only realistic way that you can make money through these currencies, speculation. I fully understand the irony of one of the advantages of digital currencies being a lack of outside speculation, but that is only true in *theory*. In our current climate most currencies cannot actually be used for goods and services. For people like you and me, the next few years of profit will be made from gaining a cryptocurrency, holding onto that currency, and then selling it at a later time.

Thinking about cryptocurrencies as gold is a good way to understand how you will be making your money. Gold isn't worth anything unless you trade it for a currency that can be used to buy goods and services. If you purchased gold one hundred years ago, you would be making quite a sizeable profit. The difference here though is that cryptocurrencies gain in value much faster than gold. You don't have to wait a long period of time for a currency to double or triple in value. At the same time, these currencies can decline in value just as quickly. The last chapter of this book will address the timing for when to buy and sell cryptocurrencies, but for right now know that the most realistic way for you to make money off of any cryptocurrencies is to get some, hold it, and sell it later.

Obtaining a Cryptocurrency

There are two basic ways to obtain any cryptocurrency, you can either buy it using traditional government backed currencies or you can create it yourself. I *highly* suggest that you mine these currencies yourself. For buying any cryptocurrency, you will have to work through a number of odd resources, specific to the currency that you choose to buy. At the end of this chapter I outline the best currencies worth investing in right now, specifically for the beginner investor. With all of the difficulty in how to obtain these currencies through traditional purchasing, you really have to mine cryptocurrencies to make an impressive profit. I thought that I was too late to start mining, but the truth is that recent advances in the power/wattage use in computer parts makes it quite reasonable to mine Bitcoin or any other cryptocurrency. None of these currencies are so far advanced that mining is impossible. With all currencies it is still profitable to start mining them yourself.

Mining

There is one last technical aspect of how Bitcoins and other cryptocurrencies that has not been discussed yet – how they are created. Right now you are aware that they are 'mined' but what does this really mean? In essence, mining is supposed to simulate the difficulty in going into the ground and searching for rare Earth metals. Like with gold, it is supposed to be easy to find currency in the beginning, but gradually it will get more difficult over time. How this type of backbreaking labor is simulated with cryptocurrencies is quite interesting – it involves computers running thousands of complicated calculations in order to *bid* on the creation of some fraction of a cryptocurrency. The equations that are being solved have no practical benefit to anyone. These are equations that are made up to purposefully be difficult for a computer to compute. This is the easiest way to simulate the labor intensive work it takes to unearth gold. When the currency is created, it is immediately deposited in the account of the miner that solved the final equation and was able to create the coin. In the next chapter I'll walk you through how you can make a machine that mines cryptocurrencies, but in essence you are paying for the cost of electricity *now* to create currency *later*. You will be making profit from selling these coins at a later time. The cost to produce these coins is always going to be lower than what they end up selling for. The market fluctuates heavily but if you time it right, you can make a lot of money from selling any cryptocurrency.

The 'chain' in blockchain refers to more than just the storage of transactions in the chain. I described in chapter one that anyone can trace the history of a single Bitcoin through it's inception to its latest owner, though the owner stays anonymous. The blocks in a blockchain also denote when a new coin in produced, in addition to the transmission of this currency. Keep in mind the core tenets of cryptocurrency and the idea of a decentralized currency. In this idea is how the creation of individual coins for these currencies was created. It is to my advantage that I claim that I created the latest Bitcoin produced. At the same time, it is to the advantage of every additional miner that they also claim they made the latest Bitcoin. The blockchain in conjunction with the solved equations proves who the actual creator is, and all members of a cryptocurrency network must agree on who created the coin. Since all members are competing against each other, we end up with a fair system in which no one is at an advantage compared to any other member. This is how we end up with a fair system in the creation of coinage for cryptocurrencies.

A Trouble Spot You Need to Be Made Aware Of

There are numerous cryptocurrencies on the market today. The technology for all of these currencies relies on blockchain, and fundamentally they function in a similar manner. There are some key differences in terms of the hashing system between these currencies. Think about each hash as a bit of stored information referring to the creation of a coin. Newer currencies were designed with hashing systems that will last long into the future. Some older currencies however are starting to run into some trouble, namely Bitcoin.

For any part of the Bitcoin protocol to change, the entire community would have to agree to a new rule set. It is extremely unlikely that in the near future the Bitcoin protocol will change, but it is something that investors need to be made aware of. Right now there is a limit to how the hashing system will work, meaning that it is going to be difficult to produce new coins in the future, or rather, it will be more difficult than originally designed. There have been new proposals for how a new hashing system would work, but the problem comes in having everyone agreeing on adopting a new system. This is what I want you to be aware of: a new hashing protocol for any cryptocurrency might give a specific advantage to certain individuals. As such, be on the lookout for changes to the hashing system for cryptocurrencies; if there is news that a new system is to be adopted, it might be worth cashing out of that particular cryptocurrency. There are inherit risks to sticking around with a new hashing system, and it is a concern for many analysts looking at the current market for these currencies.

Good Cryptocurrencies for Beginners

There are a number of cryptocurrencies on the market. Below are the ten most popular ones based on market capitalization. The market cap for these coins is based on a simple calculation of what the average coin is selling for multiplied by the total number of coins that have been produced. The market cap essentially provides the total value for any currency if the entire inventory were to be made liquid. Realistically, these values are off by quite a bit. If someone tried to sell a large amount of Bitcoin, it would drop the average price of a single coin, therefore altering the equation and adjusting the market cap. Knowing this, there are multiple things that need to be taken into account to select the proper cryptocurrencies for investment. Of the top ten currencies, anything marketed with an asterisk (*) is a currency that I would recommend to beginners. These are currencies that either look promising based on their improved hashing system (protocol disputes won't be a problem in the future) or they have been proven currencies. Bitcoin is a tricky one; it's a proven currency that has been around for years, but it the most difficult to mine since it is the most matured. If you are starting today, my bet would be on Nxt or MaidSafeCoin – these both have a good intersection of reliable protocols and a healthy user base supporting these currencies. I particularly like Nxt and believe that it will prove to be a major player in the future. Currencies like Ripple and Bitshares are harder to recommend. They are so closely based on Bitcoin but don't come with the same prestige. They represent the worst of both worlds, harder to mine and don't provide the best hashing protocols moving forward. Ideally you will have several machines that mine in different currencies.

If I only had two machines for mining, I would focus on Nxt and Bitcoin. Three machines and I would add in MaidSafecoin. Four machiens and I would add Litecoin to that list. You want a good mix of established currencies and new currencies that are on the cutting edge of blockchain technology. Remember that you are making an investment, and as such you will want to diversify your holdings.

1. Bitcoin*
2. Ripple
3. Litecoin*
4. Bitshares
5. Darkcoin
6. Nxt*
7. Dodgecoin
8. MaidSafeCoin*
9. Stellar
10. Paycoin

Chapter 4: Mining for Beginners

An Introduction to Mining

I believe mining is the best way to realize the most profit from digital currencies. You can buy cryptocurrencies, but the cost of creating your own is quite low. By creating your own notes, your able to make a greater profit because the value you are adding to the economy is the in the production of these coins. If you just buy and sell coins then you are merely becoming a speculator. Granted, speculation is the main factor in why these coins increase in value, but the argument still stands that the most money can be made from mining coins instead of buying them.

The hashing system that creates new coins for cryptocurrencies is complicated, but getting your own system up and running is actually quite easy. All you need is a computer and free software that can be found on the respective cryptocurrency's website. For example, to mine Bitcoin all you need is the free Bitcoin software available at Bitcoin.org. You simply boot up the miner, pay the cost of electricity, and then collect the occasional coin or fraction of a coin that you produce. This alone is not going to net you enough of any one cryptocurrency to make you wealthy; to do that you will need to understand the best practices for making best use of electricity to create these coins.

Dedicated to Mining

Any computer that you use for mining should be used, and only used, for mining. For example, if you've ever received a virus in the last few years that slowed down your computer, you may have noticed that other than this slowdown, it wasn't all that invasive in terms of causing pop-up messages, stealing your data or causing other problems. This is because a lot of popular malware that is created today is made with the express intent of creating a digital currency. The creator or distributor of the malware will want to infect as many computers as possible, and use the shared resources from all of these computers to solve the equations that will net them digital currency. It's actually pretty clever, but at the same time is not all that effective. That is because most computers on the market today ship without a GPU, or graphics processing unit. Most computers these days are in fact laptops and most only use CPUs, or central processing units. I understand that when it comes to computer hardware, it is not common knowledge what a CPU or GPU does. That's fine; you don't actually need to know that much about computers to get a mining rig up and running. Just understand that what makes or breaks a mining rig is the power of its graphics processor. Since laptops typically don't have these, they simply cannot create cryptocurrencies as easily. While there are laptops that come with GPUs, these are prohibitively expensive and require purchasing the entire unit directly from the manufacturer. This is why I suggest that you make assemble your own mining rig.

The idea of assembling your own computer can seem quite scary, but the truth isn't nearly that bad. A simple search on YouTube and there are hundreds of instructional tours for how to assemble a computer once you have each and every component. In all honesty, it's a lot like assembling Mega Blocks or Lego. The pieces fit together nicely and once you understand what components you want to buy, creating your first mining rig is a process that takes less than three or four hours. First, let's review the equipment that you need, as well as giving a brief description of each component. To create a mining rig, you are going to need six basic components: motherboard, central processing unit, RAM or memory, graphics processing unit, power supply, and storage. I am omitting all unnecessary components, including the case of a computer – if you are mining and building your own computer, I would actually advise against a case; it's just unnecessary for a stationary machine that will never be moved.

The Motherboard

The motherboard is the component that ties together all other components in your mining rig. You connect all the other components on this list to this component. The cost of motherboards range greatly, from lows of $40 to highs of several hundred dollars. You don't need a fancy motherboard to build a mining rig. You just need to make sure that it is *full sized* and not the *micro* version. The best suppliers of reliable motherboards are ASUS, GIGABIT, and Intel. If you buy a motherboard from any one of these companies for $70-$80, you are looking at a board that will last you many years.

It's important to note, that the motherboard is going to determine the type of CPU and memory that is able to be slotted in. Motherboards are designed for one type of CPU and one type of memory. You simply need to ensure that the motherboard type is the same as the CPU type that you are going to slot in. There are utilities that will show compatibility problems between components, and almost always this is just an issue with the wrong motherboard. Before you buy anything, I suggest you use PCPartPicker.com to look for compatibility issues in your mining rig.

CPU

The CPU, or central processing unit, is one of the two computation pieces on your mining right. This is the component that will attempt to handle long form calculations for mining if you do not have a graphics processor present. This is where the calculations are handled on most laptops for example. This component should be a mid tier processor, as it hands instructions over to the graphics processor for which equations need to be processed. It therefore can be the limiting factor if you decide to buy one that is too slow. I suggest that you purchase an Intel CPU (the alternative being AMD) and go with any recent i5 processor. The way that Intel breaks down their processor line is they come in three variants, with the i5 sitting squarely in the middle. You can expect this component to come in at around $200-$300 and should last for a minimum of four years of continuous mining if the computer is on 24/7.

RAM, or Memory

The RAM, or random access memory, of the computer does not matter that much for mining. You will want to ensure that you have compatible RAM with your motherboard, but aside from this there is little difference between brands and channel speeds. You will want to have at least 4gb of ram, and you can expect this to cost you around $40, but is variable depending on the type of motherboard that you buy. For example, an older motherboard will allow for the DDR3 type which is slightly older and cheaper than the newer DDR4. The upper limit for the cost of this component is $90.

GPU

This is the most important component in any cryptocurrency mining rig. It is also one of the first components that will burn out. You are going to be running this piece of equipment at full intensity 24/7, and can only expect around two years of usage, maybe three depending on how many tips you follow in the next chapter. The graphics processing unit is commonly used to play graphics intensive computer games, but the reason why it's so useful in mining is because of its architecture. This unit features many dozens of small processors, not all that different from a CPU, that run at a lower speed. It means that no single calculation can be done as quickly as the computer's CPU, but that many calculations can be done in parallel. If you think about how coins are mined, it makes perfect sense then that this component would be so useful. You are trying to solve thousands of calculations and the power behind each processor on the GPU is powerful enough to solve any one of them. Therefore we throw as many problems at a GPU that it can possibly take and solve them all at once. Since this is such an important component, I'll break down specific models that you will want to buy in the next chapter. For now, know that this component will cost somewhere between $200-$300.

Power Supply

After the GPU, I believe that the power supply is the most important component in any mining rig. The reason is simple; your main enemy in mining is the cost that it takes to power the machine. An efficient power supply can reduce the operating costs to mine by a substantial amount. Power supplies come in five grades: titanium, platinum, gold, silver, and bronze, as well as the un-graded power supplies. You will want to get at least a silver rated power supply.

These marks correspond to the efficiency of the power supply. The more efficient a power supply is, the higher the percent of AC current it is translating to DC current for the computer. For example, if it takes 400 watts to power a mining computer, an 80% efficient power supply will need to get 500 watts to convert. That means that you are burning an additional 100 watts of energy that is being lost in the conversion. Over time, regardless of the quality of the power supply, these devices will become less efficient. These need to be replaced roughly once a year and will cost between $70 and $120. The total wattage that you should be looking for is around 500. The specific needs of your computer will range depending on the GPU, but 500 will cover just about every single common case.

As an additional note about the power supply and why you don't want to buy the cheapest option: these components can destroy your entire system. The information that I'm providing to you is based on my own experience with learning how to mine. My first assembled rig had an unrated power supply and worked just fine for about four months. Aside from raking up additional power costs (something I wasn't closely paying attention to in the beginning), when these components break, they have the potential to take the entire computer with it. In my case it burned out the CPU, GPU and motherboard. The most expensive pieces of equipment were destroyed because when the coils on the power supply broke, they provided far too much current to the individual components in the computer, causing all of them to short. In addition, when this piece breaks it can actually burst into flames; this is especially dangerous if you aren't monitoring your rig 24/7, which most of won't be. Go with a silver power supply at a minimum – in addition to providing better conversion efficiency, when this grade of power supply breaks, it's not going to take other components with it. Simply, the higher rated power supplies break much more 'cleanly' than the cheap ones.

Storage

The last component that you will need for your mining rig is a storage device. This is where the operating system and all of the local hashing information about the cryptocurrency is located. You'll want something reliable, but not something that is overly expensive and on the cutting edge. Right now you have two basic options, either a mechanical hard drive (HDD) or a solid state drive (SSD). SSDs use less power than HDDs, but they are far more expensive. I would simply use HDDs and expect to pay around $40 per drive. The amount of storage you need is not much, and anything over 100 GB will have you covered.

For what it is worth, you likely cannot buy a HDD with such little storage, and will likely have to buy a 500 GB or 1 TB drive instead.

Your Operating System

The components above are good for a single mining rig, but then there is the issue of the operating system that will be running the software that mines. You should not pay for the operating system of your mining rig/s. I say this because the open source nature of cryptocurrencies has shown a great amount of support for open source operating systems. This means that you should be installing Linux on your mining rig. There are many version of Linux, with some minor changes across versions. I still use 'Red Hat', but any current version is suitable. This can be downloaded from a variety of websites that host the operating system. You simply need to download the operating system and load it onto a flash drive to install it on your storage device.

The Equipment You Think You Need but Can Do Without

I have listed six items that you need to purchase and one that is entirely free. You may look at this list and think that there are obvious omissions, but remember that we are not building a computer for daily personal use. We are building machines specific to a single task. You will need internet connectivity to connect to any cryptocurrency network but this network connection is located on every motherboard. It will not be a wireless card, but will allow you to plug your computer directly into your modem or router. Other components like mouse, keyboard, speakers and monitor are either unnecessary or can be used across multiple computers. You shouldn't' be buying a monitor for each mining rig that you have, for example. You would just plug in any rig that you want to configure at that time. If you don't have a monitor that you can currently use, that's fine too, you can just use any HDTV as modern GPUs have HDMI ports. It's not an ideal way to use the computer day to day, but it's fine for the purpose of mining. Speakers are completely unnecessary and shouldn't even be connected, meanwhile a mouse and keyboard is either something that you have lying around, or you should just buy the cheapest version that you can, and used if possible. You shouldn't spend more than $20 at the very most for a mouse and keyboard. The key to mining is to reduce the costs of getting each and every coin from a cryptocurrency network, therefore look for where you can cut corners. The six components that I have listed above are the most important, and even here you can see that some parts are more essential than others Go with what you *need* and remember the purpose for why you are building a rig at all – it is a means to an end and not something that is supposed to be used recreationally or daily.

Chapter 5: Tips and Strategies for Mining

Your Number One Enemy is Electricity
There is a single cost to mining other than the cost of the hardware and the time it takes to assemble each rig. Your main enemy is going to be the cost of electricity. While electricity might be cheap where you live, the machines that you will be building will add a fairly substantial cost to your electric bill each and every month. Therefore, to get the most profit out of your mining machines, you will need to ensure that they are running as efficiently as possible.

In the last chapter I outlined the basic type of hardware that you will need to build your mining rig. In that chapter I mentioned the power supply and the efficiency rating associated with these units. This is the type of thinking that you will have to take to how your mining rigs operate from moment to moment. Since these machines are running 24/7, any reduction in operating costs will make a huge difference in your profit margin. Some of these tips are more difficult to invoke than others, but try and work in the areas that you can and you will see your profits climb ever higher.

Consider Your Cooling Solution
A basic principle of computing is that the cooler a component is running, the less electricity it consumes. With more heat comes greater power requirements, and so you will want to make sure that you are cooling your mining rig is running as efficiently as possible. I have two pieces of advice on this topic: one, do not try and cool your machines using methods that you would use to cool yourself or you home and two, invest in good thermal paste and cooling units for your CPU and GPU.

I see a lot of early miners running their home's air conditioning on full blast trying to cool down their mining equipment. This is literally the worst way to try and cool off a computer for the purposes of reducing cost. The ambient temperature of a room matters for the temperature of individual components, but not nearly as much as you might think. The cost of running an air conditioner is far greater than what you save from the heat on computer parts. In truth, up to around eighty-five degrees Fahrenheit, you don't need to worry about the temperature where your mining rig is. These machines get really hot as it is, and a ten degree difference in temperature is absolutely nothing compared to the savings that you would receive from better thermal paste or cooling unit.

Thermal paste is the connector between a processor and the cooling unit mounted on top of that processor. It conducts the heat away from the processor and into the air around the unit. When you buy a CPU, it comes with some thermal paste, but it is the cheapest paste available. You are better off spending around $20 for a container of Artic Silver thermal paste. This can be used many times over can have a significant effect on the overall temperature that your processor operates at. In addition to thermal paste, also consider the cooling units that get mounted on top of the thermal paste. The stock, or standard, cooling unit available for GPUs will generally be just fine. However the stock units for CPUs are typically quite poor. You have many options for how to cool a CPU and all different price points, but what I have found is that efficiency tops out at round the $30 price point. An 'air' cooler of this cost is perfect for a CPU and will reduce costs quite a bit. There is also the option of 'water' cooling your mining rig; I advise against this because of the complexity of setup, the cost of this type of cooling and the maintenance required. A slightly better than stock cooling unit is more than enough for your CPU, and the stock cooler on any GPU will be just fine.

The Dangers of Static

This tip is not so much designed around power efficiency, as much as ensuring that you do not ruin any hardware as you are installing it. All computer components are vulnerable to being shorted due to static discharge. There are some simple things that you can do to ensure that you do not break any components as you are installing them. For one, make sure that your workspace is not carpeted and that you are not wearing socks. Carpet and socks are great at getting static to build up in the body, and even if you do not feel a *shock*, it is still possible to short a component if you aren't careful. Second, make sure you ground yourself before handling any component. This can be done simply enough by touching something metal near you. Simply touch a metal object then you can interact with a component knowing that you are grounded and not in risk of shorting a component. Third, you can optionally buy an anti-static wristband. This is a band that you wear and attach to a grounded object in your home. It essentially keeps you grounded at all times so you don't have to worry about shorting any components. Personally, I would go with option three here. I waited far too long to get an anti-static band, and while I've never shorted any components before, it's really nice being able to work without having to worry about breaking a part due to static.

Selecting the Right GPU

The single most power intensive unit in your mining right will be your GPU. It is important that you buy the most recent iteration of graphics processing units for your mining rig, as the jumps made in power efficiently makes them a no-brainer purchase. Right now you have two good options for mid-range graphics cards that are prefect for mining. There is the AMD 480 and the Nvidia

1060. Either model here, prices at $200 and $250 respectively, is a great purchase for mining. Some will argue that you should string multiple of these units together in a single rig, however I would advise against doing this to start. A single one of either of these cards will do a fine job of mining.

You may have noticed one of the GPUs I've recommended comes from one of the two major manufactures of CPUs. You should note that all video cards are compatible with any CPU and any other component. The only time you really need to look for a compatibility issue is between the motherboard and the ram and CPU. There will never be a conflict if you install either one of these cards.

Dust

The number one driver of heat in your mining rig will be the dust that the computer components attract. Once every two weeks you need to dust your computer components using compressed air. Personally, I invested in a special vacuum for cleaning up dust on computer parts. This vacuum was only $40 or so, and you will notice that the amount of compressed air you go through will make this a worthwhile purchase. Regardless of how you clean dust out of your rig, make sure that it is relatively clean to get the most out of the components.

Reduce the Upfront Cost

There are some components on your mining rig that you will need to spend a decent amount of money on. Those components are the CPU, GPU and power supply. Either these components start at relatively high prices or you will want to get a very reliable unit. All other components in your computer can be very low grade parts however, and you shouldn't be afraid to buy used. I would certainly look around Craigslist for common parts like mouse, keyboard and monitor, but also for parts like RAM and HDDs. Any cost reductions up front will spell a great profit for you when you sell your cryptocurrencies. These parts will typically either work or they don't; they don't slowly break over time (with the exception of HDDs and power supplies), so feel free to buy used as long as it works. You won't be receiving a product that will last as long, but while it works, it will work just as well as any equivalent unit.

Chapter 6: Calculating Your Profit and Knowing When to Sell Your Holdings

The Hard Truth About Cryptocurrencies

I am a supporter of blockchain based currencies; I think it is an incredible technology with a lot of practically and functionality over traditional currencies. That being said, I need to be realistic about the future of *all* independent blockchain currencies. At some point in the future, a government will adopt a blockchain based currency and will render all existing private currencies obsolete. Right now, the value of blockchain based currencies is in their novelty and the potential for how they can change how financial transactions are done in the future. If a government were to adopt blockchain technology in their own currency, it would spell the end for independent non-state affiliated currencies. There is of course the potential that a government could back one of the major currencies, but this just seems unrealistic because it is wholly unnecessary. What we have seen in the last few years is that the technology is there, and that all that is necessary is the will to create a new currency. The moment a large government wants to create currency on par with Bitcoin, it can do so almost immediately, and it would be far more useful to the average consumer as it could be used in stores an deposited in regular bank accounts.

This is a very pessimistic view on the future of cryptocurrencies, but that does not dissuade me from mining today. I know that I will make plenty of profit between now and the time that these currencies are no longer sustainable or of interest to investors. The key is to do the timing just right – you need to exit the market at regular intervals, meaning sell the inventory that you have when the price is at the right value. Fro example, the price of Bitcoin recently crossed over $1000. This is when I decided to sell my current inventory of Bitcoin. The moment Nxt hits a new high, I'll sell my reserves of that currency as well. My point here is that you need to be realistic about where this currency is going in the long haul. This is not something that you should leave in your will to your grand children. These cryptocurrencies operate on a much smaller time frame, and you will need to cash out at regular intervals to ensure your profits. This brings us to the final topic I wish to discuss, calculating your profit.

Calculating Your Profit

I've made just about $30,000 mining in the last two years. It's not my primary income, however I am working on building more machines to increase my total profit. My calculations for how I determined that my profit was $30,000 were not simple. I had to keep track of all of my electric bills for the last two years, and run adjustments to see what the added cost of my mining hardware was on my standard utility bill. I had to keep meticulous track of all of the money that I have spent on hardware over the last two years to run my mining rigs. With this information though, I was able to accurately calculate the total profits that I have made from cryptocurrencies. This is my final word of advice to you – keep track of everything that you do in regards to this type of investing. The only way to calculate your profit in any sort of accurate way is going to be keeping track of all of your expenses. After this difficult step, all you have to do to calculate profit is factor in how much you were able to sell your digital currencies for. To reiterate, I am firm believer that profit can be made from cryptocurrencies, but you have to be realistic about where this profit is going to come from. It's not going to come from simply the rise in value of a cryptocurrency, because the likelihood that it can ever be exchanged for a wide array of goods and services is slim to none. You will have to exchange it at regular intervals for government backed currency. This is the only way to realize profits; you can't bet on these currencies being around forever, but don't let that stop you from making real money right now.

Conclusion

Thank you again for downloading *Blockchain: The Industry Leader's Guide to Blockchain, Understanding Bitcoin and Entering the Digital Economy*.

You are now ready to hit the ground running and get invested in cryptocurrencies. It may seem that the time has passed for these cryptocurrencies, but that is far from the truth. Digital currencies have many years left of viability before they fade away, and if you get invested now, you can earn good profit from mining an assortment of different blockchain based currencies. I hope that I have shown you how easy and affordable it is to produce your own mining computer. You know what you need to do and now you just need to get to action and before long you will be able to start selling currency and collecting your profits.

Your first step is to start assembling your mining rig and decide on what currency you are gong to first mine. If I were starting in early 2017, I would choose Nxt as my first currency to mine. If you start now, by the end of 2017 you should be able to make a decent amount of profit from just a single mining machine working on this currency. As time goes on, I hope that you build additional mining rigs and work on the efficiency in which they operate. Remember that the electric company is the enemy, and that you can refer to chapter five to reduce your operating costs.

If you are still unsure about your future in cryptocurrencies and mining, I implore you to take a few months and follow the trends of any of the major currencies. You will see patterns in the rise and fall of the market cap and average sale price of a single denomination of any one of these digital currencies. If you are truly just trying to test the waters, buy some Nxt and Bitcoin and see if you can make profit as the prices rise over time. You will see that there are certainly wild price fluctuations, but that this is a revolution that is not going away anytime soon. Detractors claimed that Bitcoin would never surpass $1000 per coin again, and yet late in 2016 Bitcoin did exactly that. I highly suggest that you get involved in mining, but if your only entry point is to buy into a currency wholesale, that is a better alternative to sitting on the sidelines and watching this digital revolution pass you by.

Lastly if you enjoyed this book, it would be much appreciated if you could leave a review on Amazon. The best way for this book to make its way into the hands of more readers is through truthful reviews about this work. Please write what you liked about this book and what could be improved upon. Any and all feedback is helpful as I continue to serve the needs of my readership.

Thank you and good luck!

www.ingramcontent.com/pod-product-compliance
Lightning Source LLC
Chambersburg PA
CBHW070731180526
45167CB00004B/1711